Flowers

This edition 2003

Franklin Watts
96 Leonard Street
London EC2A 4XD

Franklin Watts Australia
45-51 Huntley Street
Alexandria
NSW 2015

Copyright © 1993 Franklin Watts
Editor: Ambreen Husain
Design: Volume One

A CIP catalogue record for this book is available from
the British Library.
Dewey Decimal Classification Number: 582.13

ISBN: 0 7496 5261 6

Printed in Hong Kong/China

Photographs: Heather Angel 13, 18, 26; Bruce
Coleman Ltd (E Crichton) 7 inset, 11, 14, 15,
(J Grayson) 9, (J Cowan) 21, (C Wallace) 22-23,
(K Taylor) 27, (P Ward) 28, (J Burton) 29,
(D Orchard) 30; DLP Photo Library (David Heald)
8; Eye Ubiquitous (P Claydon) 16, (J Northover) 17,
(K Oldroyd) 24, cover; Chris Fairclough Colour
Library 5, 6, 25; NHPA (L Campbell) 12; Oxford
Scientific Films (H Fox) 10, (S Osolinski) 19;
Photo Horticultural 7; Kenneth Scowen 20, 31.

WALKABOUT
Flowers

Henry Pluckrose

W
FRANKLIN WATTS
LONDON•SYDNEY

Flowers seem to grow
almost everywhere.
These woodland flowers
are wild.
They grow wherever
there is warmth,
sunlight, water
and soil.

Garden flowers grow
where we plant them.
They also need warmth,
sunlight, water and the
soil in which to grow.

Flowers grow from seeds,
bulbs or corms.
If we plant these seeds
in the spring,
each will grow into a
flowering plant by summer.

If we plant these bulbs
in the autumn,
each will grow into
a spring flower.

Plants have roots
which push down into the soil.
The roots find the water
and the chemicals in the soil
which the plant needs.

The leaves of a plant
contain a green pigment
called chlorophyll.
The leaves use the chlorophyll
and sunlight to make food.
They turn the water and
chemicals collected by the roots
into sugar.
Sugar is the food
which the plant needs to live.

There are many kinds of flower.
Each kind of flower
has its own special shape.
The petals on this pansy
are round and flat.

Some, like these lilies, look rather like a trumpet.

Others are umbrella-shaped

or round like a ball,

narrow and pointed

or simply spiky!

There are flowering plants
which are bushes

and flowering plants which climb.

There are flowers which grow in water

and flowers which
can grow in places
that are hot and dry.

There are flowers
which grow on trees

and flowers which grow in walls.

There are flowers
in many colours
and flowers of different sizes.

But why do plants
need to flower?

Each flower head
contains new life . . .
seeds for next year's plants.
To make the seeds grow
they must be fertilized
with pollen from another plant
of the same kind.

Every flower contains nectar.
Nectar is a sweet smelling liquid.
Bees, butterflies and other insects
collect the nectar
from inside the flower.

As the bee moves down inside the flower to drink the nectar, pollen from the flower sticks onto its legs.

The bee carries this pollen
with it from plant to plant . . .
and fertilizes the seeds.
Can you see the yellow pollen?

When the flower dies,
the seeds which have
been fertilized
begin to grow and ripen.
This is the seed case
of the poppy.

Where there was once a dandelion flower there is now a head of tiny seeds.

We grow flowers in our parks and gardens,
in pots and window boxes . . .
and even in huge fields.

Do you have
a favourite flower?

About this book

Young children acquire much information in an incidental, almost random fashion. Indeed, they learn much just by being alive! The books in this series complement the way in which young children learn. Through photographs and a simple text the readers are encouraged to comment on the world in which they live.

To the young child, life is new and almost everything in the world is of interest. But interest alone is not enough. If a child is to grow intellectually this interest has to be harnessed and extended. This book adopts a well tried and successful method of achieving this end. By focusing upon a particular topic, it invites the reader firstly to look and then to question. The words and photographs provide a starting point for discussion. Discussion also involves listening. The adult who listens to the young reader's observations will quickly realise that children have a very real concern for the environmental issues that confront us all.

Children enjoy having information books read to them just as much as stories and poetry. The younger child may ignore the written words ... pictures play an important part in learning, particularly if they encourage talk and visual discrimination.

Henry Pluckrose